MW01250723

Teach for Souls

A Christian Discussion Worth Having

Clinton Taylor

authorHOUSE®

AuthorHouse™
1663 Liberty Drive
Bloomington, IN 47403
www.authorhouse.com
Phone: 1-800-839-8640

First published by AuthorHouse   7/6/2009

ISBN: 978-1-4389-8932-7 (e)
ISBN: 978-1-4389-8748-4 (sc)

Printed in the United States of America
Bloomington, Indiana

This book is printed on acid-free paper.

Contents

Introduction   vii

Chapter One
The Heartbeat of God   1

Chapter Two
What Does It Mean To Be Lost?   5

Chapter Three
The Great Commission, Not the Great Suggestion   11

Chapter Four
Book of Books   17
Book of Books Questions   24

Chapter Five
The Question of God   25
The Question of God Questions   31

Chapter Six
The Problem of Sin   33
The Problem of Sin Questions   43

Chapter Seven
Who is Jesus Christ?   45
Who is Jesus Christ? Questions   55

Chapter Eight
The Plan for Salvation   59
The Plan for Salvation Questions   77

Chapter Nine
Benefits and Consequences   81
Benefits and Consequences Questions   83

Conclusion   89

INTRODUCTION

I am truly excited to be able to share this simple, yet essential Bible study discussion with you. My enthusiasm stems from the reality of the times we are living in. As I traverse the different areas of my community and various other places, I find—almost on a daily basis—people of all nationalities, races, and genders who are seeking spiritual fulfillment. I am aware of this because, when I approach many of them, they are filled with questions about God, the Bible, and their purpose for being here on the Earth.

I find this to be magnificent because such encounters give me—an individual who enjoys talking about God—the opportunity to do just that with them. However, during some of my talks with many of these people, I would find that I was at times unable to bring them to a point where they would express faith and begin a relationship with the Lord. After many years of experiencing this kind of set back in helping people to learn about God and to receive Him, I discovered a huge error that I was constantly making. My error was simply that I seemed to spend more time preaching and trying to convince those that I spoke with about spiritual truths, instead of doing what Jesus did, when He shared the message of faith and salvation.

When Jesus wanted to communicate spiritual truths, He would often do so by using two effective methods: First, He would share the message of faith and salvation with people many times one on one; and secondly, He would enter into meaningful discussions with them. He did not rely on using the style of mouthing off an overabundance of scripture on various religious topics; but rather, Jesus took the time to sit and talk with people while posing and answering questions that would eventually lead them to faith and knowledge about God.

We see this style of presentation frequently in the New Testament. The following three illustrations are great examples of this: the book of John records Jesus' conversation with Nicodemus (John 3:1-21) and his encounter with the woman at the well (John 4:7-38); and the book of Acts describes Priscilla and Aquila's experience with Apollos (Acts 18:24-25). The huge and evident benefit of sharing the Gospel of Jesus Christ in this way (a discussion) is that, by doing so, you are truly able to explain the Word of God to those whom you are working with in a timely manner. In the end, you will help to produce a true convert—not someone who is forced or brain-washed into believing in Jesus Christ and becoming a Christian.

This is my primary motivation in creating this Bible discussion. *Teach for Souls* is designed to be used by people who have already accepted Christ, and truly is a tool that will assist believers in familiarizing themselves with sharing the Gospel through an organized presentation of the Word of God. The first four chapters are written to the believer showing the need for evangelism. This is followed by a Bible discussion outlining six different topics that people commonly have questions about. I will start off by showing that in fact there the Bible is the Word of God and then showing that there is a God who can be personally known.

Then we will look at the problem of sin, revealing how men became sinners, while showing that this problem of sin is a universal one that only Jesus Christ can take care of. This is followed by our discussion about who Jesus Christ really is, and then God's plan for getting men freed from sin. This final discussion will outline the benefits for accepting the salvation message as well as the negative consequences for rejecting it.

I trust and pray you will find *Teach for Souls* to be a simple yet comprehensive tool that you will be able to use in your soul-winning endeavors. I encourage you to employ its principles while God is still blessing us with the gift of life here on earth to share His Gospel.

CHAPTER ONE

The Heartbeat of God

Have you ever stopped for a moment to consider what God may be doing in Heaven on any particular day? I mean, what does God do all day long? Does He just sit in Heaven on His throne and look at humans as they go about their daily lives? For starters, we know that He does not sleep (Psalms 121:4) and that He does not get bored. So what does He do then with His time? What things are most important to Him? What could possibly rest in His heart to the point that it might bother Him or perhaps even move Him to action? I hope I am not being seen as irreverent by asking these questions, but realistically, we all have asked questions like these—questions that puzzle us from time to time about God.

Of all of these questions, one question in particular would continuously burden me—the troublesome question of the things that God considers important. Well, the answer to my question would eventually come and it brought with it both a great revelation and a life -long assignment that has changed my life tremendously.

One afternoon during prayer, I mustered up enough courage to ask, "Lord, what's on Your heart today?" I didn't know what to expect after asking this question. To be honest, I wasn't expecting a response that would be profound at all. I thought that God might perhaps say, "You are on My mind" or "The Church is on My heart today"; you know, something cute that would give me a warm, fuzzy feeling. I anticipated some kind of an assurance that would strengthen me and help me in my daily journey with Him. Was I ever wrong!

To my amazement, the Lord shared with me a snapshot of what was on His heart each day. Now before I go any further, let me say that I am not one who likes to run with the words "the Lord told me". I take tremendous care when I step forward to represent the Lord in anything that I do. I tremble at the idea of saying "God said". This is due to my understanding of what the Bible has to say about those false and self-serving 'prophets' who would say things using the name of the Lord knowing that Lord had not spoken to them, nor has He called on them to represent Him in any public way.

During this experience, the Lord impressed this truth upon my heart, that the most important matter on His heart is world evangelism. I paused for a brief moment to ponder what I was receiving. I always knew that evangelism (reaching out to the unsaved) was vital, but I guess I had not seen it as the most important matter on the heart of God. I can remember thinking to myself that day, what about prayer, or giving, or even better, what about protecting the Church from its enemies, both those external and internal? I quickly realized that although those things were important, they were not necessarily the most important priorities for Jesus Christ.

As I began to listen to the Lord and to pray for a clearer understanding of what I was receiving, I witnessed as it were a sea of people appear before me. These people were seemingly from every nation under Heaven. There were laughing, talking, and walking, and having 'a great time' but as I looked more intently, they were heading directly into a gigantic lake. They apparently were not privy to the fact that they were heading in the direction of this lake until they actually got there, but once they get there, there was no turning back.

You see, as there people were laughing, talking, and walking, they were being cajoled into believing that they were on right track of life and that they were heading into what they were told was their ultimate paradise. However, the truth is this: these people were all under a spell, a spell that made them believe that life was theirs to live and that they were autonomous of all other powers, even the power of God.

Now, after experiencing this encounter with the Lord that day, I spent the rest of my time with the Lord that afternoon sobbing, and trying to understand exactly what it was that the Lord wanted me to do with this information and most importantly with the rest of my life. Needless to say, my entire view of the Church and its purpose and even the purpose of life completely changed after that afternoon encounter with God.

The Lord made it clear to me, even though I had been somewhat aware of it previously, that the purpose of the Church was much more than singing, shouting, and hosting special events; we have a far greater mandate. It is our responsibility to get outside of the four walls and begin to make Jesus' presence felt in the earth. It is our responsibility also to make God's doctrine known to those who may never enter the doors of a church, irrespective of how favorable an impression we have of our churches.

This life-changing encounter with God made it clear to me that I need to reach the lost—lost souls whose eternities rest at the center of Jesus' heart.

CHAPTER TWO
What Does It Mean To Be Lost?

o you have any idea of what it really means for a man or a woman to be lost forever? Many people including myself would like to believe that they have a clear understanding of this concept of eternity. I had preached and taught for years on the need for people to receive salvation. I would explain that people needed to make Christ their Lord and Savior because they were sinners and that if their sins weren't pardoned before they died, they would be unable to enter into Heaven.

I would proclaim this truth because I believed it to be a fundamental teaching contained in the Holy Bible. However, something was greatly wrong with my Gospel presentation because I did not always take it to heart when I would see people, after they had heard the Gospel message, would leave God's presence without giving their lives over to Him. Many of these people would express to me or to others who were helping them to pray that "they were not ready to serve God", and they would seemingly give a litany of other reasons for their procrastination. When they would make such statements, I would just politely move on to next person or to conduct other 'important matters' in that service. But in retrospect, I know now how wrong I was.

These people are lost, and that did not move me to the core of my innermost being to try and perhaps convince them in a loving way to see that they needed the Lord. The Apostle Paul, when he was given the opportunity to offer Christ's message to people would proclaim it with such passion and conviction, so much to the point that Agrippa once said to Paul in (Acts 26:28) You almost persuaded me to become a Christian. We can deduce from Agrippa's statement that the Apostle Paul did not give a soft and unenthusiastic presentation of his faith and of Jesus' love.

Paul knew that Agrippa's response to Jesus' message would result in life or death, thus, he announced it unabashedly giving strong arguments just as a politician or a lawyer would in the heat of a close election campaign or at the end of a trial. If that were not the case, I do not believe that Agrippa would have used the word" persuaded" to describe his 'almost conversion'.

Previously, when I would encounter those who would procrastinate and squander the offer of their salvation, I would often remark, "They didn't want God to begin with, so why did I even bother to waste my time". But that mentality would eventually be altered during my prayer experience as mentioned before. There, I gained some knowledge of what it really means for a person to be lost.

The concept of being lost should be familiar to most, if not all of us; because we have all, at one point or another experienced what it feels like to be unable to find the address or location of a destination. In those mor   ts, we tend go down wrong streets, make wrong turns, or perhaps even stop to make a phone call all in hopes of getting back on the right path and arrive at our designed destination.

When the statement is made that a man or woman is "lost" it is not being suggested that they are physically lost but rather, it is being pointed out that they are lost in a spiritual sense. This is entirely different from being lost in the process of trying to find a special restaurant or some other geographical location. To be lost in this context carries a much superior meaning. When it is said that a person is lost, it conveys the fact that those people who are lost will spend his or her eternity (life after death) in the lake of fire, and that there in that lake of fire, they will burn forever without end.

Until a believer is able to grasp this concept, they will never truly be able to understand the urgency or the importance of evangelism which I will deal with later in this book. Jesus understood completely the concept of a person being lost. We read time and again in the New Testament where this is illustrated.

In the Gospel of Luke, Jesus confesses His purpose for coming on earth when He said, "For the Son of Man came to seek and to save that which was lost" (Luke 19:10). I would like to lift one simple yet outstanding word from this passage, the word to "seek". During His ministry on Earth, Jesus was keenly aware of the danger that existed for those who were lost; therefore, He sought them out with the intention of saving them. Jesus did not stand in a building wishing that people would come to Him, but He took the initiative and went out looking for prospects that He might be able to share the good news of the Gospel with, and was He ever successful in this brave endeavor. Jesus' philosophy was that if people would not come to Him, He would go to them and compel them to come to Him for salvation if that was needed (Luke 14:23).

Have you ever lost something that was dear to you? I am sure you have, just as I have. I once lost a little 12 year old boy on a train in Manhattan, New York and did I ever panic! Can you remember the tenacity in which you searched for that thing which was precious to you? Perhaps you searched day and night for it, retracing your every step with hopes of finding it. Well, mankind was lost because of Adam's action of disobedience, and God did not stop going after Adam until He was able to find him and offer him hope and salvation. Thankfully, He continues to do the same thing today—seeking and saving those who are lost.

Since the fall of mankind, God has been persistently pursuing human beings because He understands that if He fails to do so, they will be most miserable in their lives after death. You see, the reality is this: though all human beings will die someday and therefore, leave this physical cosmos, their souls will continue to live forever elsewhere. For those who have chosen to accept Jesus' love and salvation, they will be privileged to experience their eternal existence in the presence of God. There, they will enjoy peace and joy and will never have to fear sicknesses or death again (Revelation 21:4). On the contrary, there are those who will not be as fortunate. They will spend their eternal existence in a lake of fire apart from God simply because they have failed to make Jesus the Lord and master of their lives.

I agree that the concept of eternity is one that is difficult for human beings to fully comprehend because none of us have at any point in our temporal existence experienced eternity. We can only use our imaginations to ponder and make attempts at understanding what it would be like for someone to exist forever. It is almost impossible to fathom the reality of a person never being able to experience death while existing in a place of torments, as we are told will be the case for millions, if not billions of people at the end of the ages.

At this point, I will attempt to shed some light on how one might be able to vaguely understand the concept of eternity. I am chiefly interested in doing this as I believe that having an understanding of eternity will propel believers to move with urgency and with alacrity to complete the assignment that Christ has called them to fulfill in His Kingdom. It is also my hope that I will be able to help many Christians follow Christ's example and develop an awareness, burden and compassion for the eternal well-being of those who are facing a lost eternity. An understanding of the word *eternity* was the third eye-opening truth that was revealed to me during my time of prayer on that aforementioned afternoon.

To best illustrate this concept allow me the privilege of borrowing your imaginations for a moment. Let me begin by asking you to consider the largest country in the world—the nation of Russia. For the sake of our journey, consider all of the cities, towns, streets, oceans, and lakes that might be in this country. Now let's take this illustration a bit further. What if you and a team of people were asked to participate in a walkathon for some worthy cause that would entail you walking around the entire perimeter of Russia how long do you envisage it would take you and your team to do so? Would it even be possible for you to walk around such a gigantic country in one life time?

Now stretch your imaginations even a little bit further. Consider the largest continent in our world which we are told is Asia. Though it would not be likely for you and your team to complete this undertaking; imagine with me: How long would if take for you to walk around the continent of Asia?

Now go with me yet further and picture the entire planet. Do you suppose that you and your team could walk around the entire planet of Earth? And if you could do so, how long do you presume it would take for you and your team to accomplish this? How about the universe? Yes, from planet to planet, star to star; could you traverse it? Given the obstacles of gravity and the earth's atmosphere, it would most certainly be impossible.

Finally, imagine that the universe was an enormous metal ball and that an eagle was given the duty of wearing down that enormous metal ball by using its wings to simply brush against that universe every one thousand years. How many thousands of years do you believe it would take for that eagle to wear down that enormous metal ball down to the size of a standard tennis ball? I presume that at this time, many of you might be a bit bemused and are trying to decipher the point I am attempting to make. Or maybe, you have already figured it out and are ready to go on.

Either way, I can assure you that there is a method to my circumlocution. At the rate of one thousand years and with the tenderness of an eagle's wing it would realistically take millions of billions of years for the metal ball to be worn down to become the size of a tennis ball. Yet, once that task would have been accomplished, eternity would have just begun for the men, women, boys and girls, who have died without knowing and serving Jesus Christ.

With this kind of knowledge, one can clearly understand why the ministries of Jesus as well as the apostles were so direct and compelling. I believe that they had seen and understood what eternity meant and this knowledge both fuelled and motivated them to spend their entire lives attempting to convince men and women to turn their lives around by repenting and dedicating their lives to serving God.

CHAPTER THREE
The Great Commission, Not the Great Suggestion

In Jesus' final moments with His disciples, He shared with them the responsibility of the Great Commission. In giving the Great Commission, Jesus challenged His disciples to go out into all areas of the earth proclaiming to people of every nation the "good news" (that would be accomplished by His pending death, burial, and resurrection), as well as His second return. Jesus Christ believed so much in this act of soul-winning, so much to the point that He offered His own life on the cross in order to make it (evangelism) possible.

Not only would Jesus give His life to the cause of saving souls, but He thought it was appropriate that His disciples would do the same as well. (John 4:5-39) describes how Jesus met with the woman of Samaria who was known to be a prostitute in her community. Jesus did not use her known reputation as a means for judging her; instead Jesus shared with her what it is like to receive the Holy Spirit and become a new person having self-value and a life that is worth living. He told her that once she had taken a drink from His well of "living water" that she would never thirst again in the way that she did before.

Upon the woman's encounter with Jesus, she left all that she had at the well and immediately ran into the city and told all the people which she say what she had heard of Jesus. She implored them "to come, see a man". She knew that she was not able to fully explain all of what Jesus had shared with her, but she knew one thing and that is if she was successful in getting people to come to Jesus, He was more than able to make all things clear to them.

After this encounter with Jesus and the woman at the well, Jesus' disciples came and found Him sitting down at the well alone and thinking within themselves that He might be hungry they offered Him some food. To their amazement Jesus responded to them by telling them that He had food which they did not know about. Hearing this response the disciples thought that perhaps someone had brought Jesus something to eat while they had left Him, but Jesus made it clear about what He was referring to when He told them He had food that they did not know about.

In (verse 34), Jesus informed His disciples that His food—His purpose in life—was to do the will of the Father and to complete His earthly assignment before His time on Earth would come to an end. Jesus understood that He had a mission to fulfill, and that His assignment was to evangelize the world no matter what that might cost Him.

This is a powerful revelation because through it we see that Jesus was able to narrow down His entire existence on the earth to one common purpose. His single and sole purpose on earth was to save souls and we see this consistently throughout the Gospels. This should be true for us as believers today as well that we can come to a place in our lives that we are able to narrow down our existence to that of soul-winning. We can clearly see in the Scriptures that the responsibility of evangelism is a serious one. Evangelizing is so serious that Jesus did not suggest that His followers evangelize, but rather, He commanded them to be soul-winners.

Hence, when He gave His disciples in the Gospel the Great Commission, He gave them the command to "go". The word "*go*" suggests a command, and that is precisely what Jesus' disciples did. They did not live self-centered lives, but they went throughout all of their communities preaching and teaching and calling humanity to begin a relationship with their God.

As we read through the New Testament, we will find that there are many individuals who had given their lives over to the cause of soul-winning. Among those lives was that of the Apostle Paul who, as he went to persecute the Church in Jerusalem was converted on the road to Damascus (Acts 9:1-20). Paul's conversion was truly a powerful one, and immediately upon his encounter with Jesus, he was called upon to share the Gospel primarily to the Gentiles. In his writings to the believers of Rome, Paul confessed in (Romans 1:14-16) that he had an obligation to present the Gospel to the people of Rome, both to those who were educated and uneducated, cultured and uncultured, and even to those who were proletariats or affluent.

The burden of his commission to preach the Gospel of Christ weighed on him so greatly that he stated that he was indebted to those who were not saved. In other words, what Paul was saying was that just as a person might owe a credit card company and are obligated to pay the incurred debt, he also had a debt to pay. Because of this debt, he understood that he was obligated by divine commission to preach the Gospel and that failing to do so would put him in serious trouble with God.

In addition, Paul also mentions more about his call to evangelize the world in (1 Corinthians 9:16) where he states that necessity was laid upon him to preach the Gospel. Paul continued by saying that he would be condemned if he did not preach or evangelize the Gospel to the people who are lost. It is unfortunate that many believers do not view evangelism in this way. Perhaps the reason for this is due to the fact that when evangelism is presented it tends to be presented as a special ministry designed for those with a propensity for it. But how far from the truth this thought really is! Evangelism is not a special ministry that is designed for special people; it is a mandate for the entire Church of Jesus Christ. Every single member of Christ's body should be dedicated to this practice and should work diligently to see souls saved daily.

Next, I intend to make a bold statement about the above subject of evangelism, and I will do so with the greatest sense of humility. I say this because my view on this topic and perhaps my statements might be for many quite controversial. Jesus commanded His disciples to "go" and to preach the Gospel in the same way that He commanded them to baptize all nations. It is believed that if a person is not baptized he or she will not enter into the Kingdom of Heaven, because that would be considered as an act of disobedience against the Word of God.

Now I will ask that you think with me as we discuses this topic. If failure to be baptized is deemed to be disobedience, then isn't it also and equal act of disobedience to refuse to comply with Jesus' commission to "go" into the world and preach the Gospel? Is it possible for a person to neglect the responsibility of evangelism and at the same time view himself to be one who is an obedient child of God? No, it is in fact impossible!

Evangelism is essential to successful Christian living. Jesus stressed this time and again to those who desired to follow Him.

John is careful to note this in (John 15:1-8) where Jesus says that every branch (members of His body) who were in Him that did not bear fruit will be taken away and that those who do bear fruit will be purged so that they can continue to bear more fruit. Here we see the key for successful soul-winning and that is to abide in Jesus (having personal and intimate fellowship with Him). It is only sensible to conclude from reading these verses that those who do not participate in evangelizing, fail to do so because they are not in close fellowship with Christ.

What is even more shocking is that Jesus stated that the men and women who do not bear fruit will be taken away.

What did Jesus mean by this? What does it mean when He said that they would be taken away? I believe that perhaps Jesus was illustrating that because the reason for human existence is to impact the Kingdom with their lives, if they should fail to do so, He would thus, call them out of the earth even by death. It is important for us to all understand that we are not given longevity of life only to do our own wills. Instead we are given life so that we can reach the lost and help in the process of building the Kingdom of God.

For this reason, I strongly believe that, for those who have been continuously challenged by Christ and do not participate in evangelism, they will not make it into the kingdom of God. I believe this because Jesus told His disciples that if they loved Him, they should demonstrate their love for Him not so much by their service in a local Church, preaching, refraining from sinful habits, et cetera; but rather, through their willingness to keep His commandments (John 14:15).

It seems to me that those who work for the Devil are extremely obedient to him. They seem to fulfill his agenda which is in opposition to God's agenda. The more we see them in operation, we notice that they are bold, united, and are shameless in the evil they promote.

On the contrary, it would seem that Christians are very often ashamed of their faith which habitually causes them to be silent at times when they should be verbal about their faith in Jesus Christ. Paul said that he was not ashamed of the Gospel of Jesus Christ because he understood that the Gospel of Jesus Christ (the good news of His death, burial, and resurrection) was truly the power of God that would bring human beings to the point of salvation (Romans 1:16). As our existence on this Earth continues through the mercies of God, let us not forget what our true purpose is in this life. Let us not lose sight of what rests at the center of the heart of Jesus Christ and become so preoccupied with the details of our lives that we fail to fulfill the main mission and primary objective of the Church.

Let us be like the apostles and those in the early Church that impacted their world in such a way that those who were without salvation saw them as powerful people who turned their sinful world upside down through preaching and living the Gospel of the Lord (Acts 17:6). Let us also remember also that they impacted their world in the short span of time they were given and that they did so without compromising the integrity of Jesus' message of faith and righteousness.

CHAPTER FOUR
Book of Books

═══════════════════════════════

DISCUSSION 1

Welcome to *Teach for Souls*—one of the friendly discussions you will find on how to lead someone to truth faith in Jesus. I hope that you will have a great time speaking about the Lord Jesus with people from all walks of life, sharing with them the 'good news' of Christ and His Kingdom. Most of the headlines we read in the news media seem to constantly proclaim bad news that at times can get depressing; therefore, I am sure you will agree that it is nice to finally hear some good news that changes lives for the better!

Because this discussion will be a spiritual one, it is important that I depend heavily upon the Holy Bible and the Holy Spirit to direct me in all that is shared in this material. I will not attempt to incorporate any other tools or resources to explain spiritual truths and because of this, it is important that from the commencement of our discussion, it is established that the Bible is reliable and that it is the Word of Almighty God. It is needful that those who study the Bible are convinced of its validity because the Bible has been a debated book for many centuries. Many people who doubt the Christian faith seem to believe that the Bible cannot be trusted because they claim that it is blemished by human errors. Others believe that the Bible is simply man's opinion, while some simply conclude that it has no authority or significance in their daily lives. For that matter, they maintain that they do not have any need for the Bible or for its teachings.

The Bible, however, paints a very different picture of itself its authority. In (John 12:47-48), Jesus discusses the power and authority of His Word. This passage demonstrates that the Words of Christ carry tremendous authority. Jesus says that in the end—the time when all humans will be judged by God for the actions that they did while they lived on Earth, that they will be judged by the Words that He has spoken.

To shed a bit more light on what Jesus really meant, we can consider another passage found in (Revelation 20:11-12) where we are told by the Apostle John about the last judgment that Jesus spoke of. In this passage, John, the writer of the book of Revelation, is very descriptive in connecting the events that are to transpire on Judgment Day; he says that all people will stand before the throne of God, both those who are young and those who are old.

He then goes on to state that two books will be opened: one he refers to as the "books", and the other he calls "another book". John's reference to the term "books" is suggestive of the 66 books that make up the Bible, and the other he reveals to be the "book of life". Those people who had come back from the dead to be judged by God were judged based on what is written in the 66 books of the Bible as well as from the book that records all of their individual acts.

These accounts unmistakably show us that the Bible is important and that it does have genuine authority to instruct people on how they should live their lives.

HOW DID WE GET THE BIBLE?

This now leads me to draw attention to two questions that are frequently asked by people every day. Where did the Bible come from and, can the Bible be trusted?

These are great questions.

When we refer to the Bible, we are speaking of a vast collection of 66 books which were all inspired by God and recorded by the men whom He had entrusted with the task. History agrees that as a means of communicating His feelings, His will, His purpose and His plan, God selected nearly 42 men from completely different time periods, places, cultures, and occupations to record His Word.

These men were not supernatural beings in the least; neither did any of them possess any special characteristics. In fact, they were pretty ordinary folks in their day, but it is amazing to note that none of their writings disagree with one another! This is a beautiful truth when considering that there are 1189 chapters and 31,103 verses in the Bible. I believe that for this outcome to be possible, no honest person could deny that these men were led by a supernatural hand.

Now to answer the question of where the Bible came from, it can be made clear that the Bible came from God and not from man. Many passages in the Bible concur that this assertion is true. Let us consider a few of these passages.

In (2 Peter 1:20-21), Peter assures us that no book or teachings in the Bible came from the personal decision or by the free will of those who recorded God's Word. To better understand what Peter is conveying in this passage, I will use an illustration that I hope will help to make Peter's claim crystal clear.

I will use Moses as my first example. When Moses wrote the book of Genesis, he did not do so after instantly deciding one day that he wanted to record some historical or spiritual fact. Nor did he do so with the intention of leaving a personal legacy for people of future generations to read after he had died. Rather, when Moses recorded the book of Genesis, he did so upon being moved and inspired by the guidance of the Holy Spirit. Because of this, it is fair for Peter to state that the Bible truly is the Word of God and that God is responsible for its contents. Another passage in the Epistles underscores this truth of the Bible being the Word of God and not the words of men. Paul, in (2 Timothy 3:16), is quite explicit in stating that "all Scripture is given by the inspiration of God."

Both Peter and Paul agree that God is the author of the Christian Bible. Notice carefully that Paul does not say that some of the scriptures were inspired of God; rather he says that the entire Bible, from the book of Genesis straight through to the book of Revelation was completely given by God.

But now we must ask this important question: what does *inspiration* mean? Before giving a formal definition of the word *inspiration*, I will give an additional illustration by looking at the mechanics of a sail boat. In order for a sailboat to move on the open sea, it needs wind in order to get from point A to point B. In the same way, the men who documented God's Word needed to be inspired by the power of God imparted to them. If these men were not inspired by God, then they would not have been able to write as effectively as they did. In the same way that a sailboat cannot sail without the power of the wind, men could not record God's Word without God. I will now give a definition for the word inspiration. Inspiration is a divine influence or action performed on a person that qualifies that individual to receive and communicate a sacred revelation.

THE BIBLE CAN BE TRUSTED!

Finally, I will answer our second question: can the Bible truly be trusted? This is an important question, especially when we take into consideration the reality of the many religions in our societies that also claim their 'holy' books are God's word.

I will begin discussing this question by looking at the words of Solomon found in (Proverbs 30:5-6). Solomon makes an amazing case for the Bible by showing that the Bible stands above all other religious books and that the Bible can be trusted and thus accepted as the truth. It is believed that apart from Jesus Christ, Solomon was the wisest person to have ever lived on the Earth. He had great knowledge of all things and upon his divine encounter with God and God's Word, he declared that every single word of God is tested and is therefore pure. So to answer the question of whether or not the Bible can be trusted, the answer is yes, because not only has the Bible been tested by God; it has also been tested by man as well.

Things are tested to determine if they are safe or if they are dangerous; therefore, before God requested humanity to place their trust in His Word, He tested His own words during the creation of the earth. We see this in (Genesis 1:3) where "God said, 'Let there be light,' and there was light." When God called into being light, He did not have to wait, nor did He have to plea for it to come into being. His word was simply obeyed and light came forth immediately. This was one of the ways He tested His word.

Therefore, we humans do not have to blindly accept the Word of God to be true, but we are able to embrace it with all of our hearts because it has been tested; and after being tested, it was found to be true. David also concurs with this truth in (Psalm 12:6) where he says that God's Word is pure and thus it can be trusted because it has been "tried in a furnace". In addition to all of this, Jesus also agrees that the Bible is a book that can be trusted.

Throughout Jesus' life, He had a great deal to say about the Scripture. He seemed to capitalize upon every available opportunity to confess that the Scripture is the Word of God. He gave it this unique name in (John 10:35) where He boldly declares that the Scripture "cannot be broken". By this, Jesus is simply saying that even if people do not choose to accept the Scripture that does not render it useless, because the Word of God cannot be annulled.

When Jesus prayed in (John 17:17), He prayed that God would sanctify His followers by using His word. He declares that God's Words are true. Finally, in regard to all that has been said about the Bible, it is important to note that it is an extremely powerful book. Paul tells us about this in (Hebrews 4:12) where He says God's Word—the Bible—is alive and active. Paul tells us that because God's Word is so potent, it is thus able to divide between the human soul and spirit, and joints and marrow until it reaches and discerns the intentions of the human heart. Anything capable enough to separate the human soul and spirit has to be both powerful and supernatural.

Thus, in conclusion, when you and I are discussing the Word of God or when we are confronted with truths in the Word of God, we must remember that God's Word has supernatural authority. We can, therefore, completely trust it by obeying it and even proclaiming it to others who may have never before heard its teaching or who may not completely be inspired by it.

Discussion Question 1

THE BIBLE AND THE KORAN

oth Christians and Muslims alike believe that they have an obligation to be devoted to a holy book. Both groups also claim that their book, and not the other, is the Word of God. How can Christians be sure that the Bible, and not the Koran, is the authentic Word of God?

Book of Books Questions

1. Explain and discuss (John 12:47-48)

2. How does the above passage relate to (Revelations 20:11-12)

3. According to Peter how did we get the Bible? (2 Peter 1:20-21)

4. What does Paul tell us about the scriptures? (2 Timothy 3:16)

5. Explain and discuss (Proverbs 30:5-6)When God created the earth and all things, how did He do it? (Genesis 1:3)

6. Explain and discuss (Psalm 12:6)

7. Discuss what Jesus says about the Scriptures? (John 10:35 and John 17:17)

8. Explain and discuss (Hebrews 4:12)

CHAPTER FIVE
The Question of God

DISCUSSION 2

Our discussion will continue with examining the reality of just who God really is! When you turn your Bible to the opening book of Genesis, you will first discover the truth about the creation of the physical world, animals, and human beings. The opening words read like this: "In the beginning God created the Heaven and the earth" (Genesis 1:1). In this verse, no attempt is made by Moses—the writer of the book of Genesis–to prove the existence of God. This is so because Moses had a personal knowledge of God and as direct result of his knowledge and fellowship with God, he was able to simply state and affirm that God existed and that God is responsible for the creation of the Earth, human begins, and of all other life forms (Genesis 1:2-26) and (Jeremiah 10:11-16).

God as Creator of all things has been one of the most clearly taught truths in the Bible, yet we find that it has been continuously challenged by so many people from the past as well as people present-day skeptics. One of the major critics of this truth was Mr. Charles Darwin, who introduced a well-known theory that suggests humanity came into being though the process of evolution. Evolution is said to be the process where living things change and develop over "millions" of years.

I would like to point out that Darwin's theory is a direct attack against the teachings of the Bible, and in particular the teachings that are found in the book of Genesis which is really the seed plot of the Bible. If the book of Genesis cannot be trusted, then all other parts of the Bible must also be brought into question. As one begins to look closely at this idea of evolution, they will come to understand that it is only a theory, which means that is it an unproven hypothesis. How can someone rest their faith upon a concept which can only make a claim of being true? This is not the case of the Bible's presentation regarding the origin of all things and God as Creator; it is not presented as a mere theory, but as fact.

With an understanding that the Bible is in fact the Word of God, we can rest securely in the credibility of the Bible. It is trustworthy because it has been tried and proven over several thousands of years, and through all of this, has kept its integrity. (This we will discuss in-depth later on). As believers of God, we do not need to feel ashamed to admit our belief in Him when questions about His existence are posed. We are in possession of the greatest book, a holy book; one that does not lie, and one which can defend itself even in the most hostile of situations.

This God which Genesis introduces to the world is unlike any other! You might ask how I am able to make such a bold or some would say, narrow-minded statement considering the fact that there are so many other religious convictions present in this world. I am able to make such a bold assertion because God has proven repeatedly that He is indeed the only "true" God as we are told of in (Jeremiah 10:10). Jeremiah alludes to the fact that the God who is presented in the Bible is the "true God" and also that He is also the "everlasting King".

This is not intended to offend others who may believe in different gods or who may have different ideas about God. But throughout history, when these other gods have been put to the test, they seem to come up short in many respects because they cannot see, hear, feel, speak, and the list goes on and on. Therefore, we are able to attest to this truth that no matter how many people may choose to reject the fact that there is no god like the God of the Holy Bible.

You and I do not have to go very far to find out that there are a plethora of persons who have chosen to identify themselves as atheists, meaning that they do not believe in the existence of God or any so-called higher power for that matter. Their argument is that people who are "intelligent" will not believe in someone or in something that they are unable to see, touch, hear, and so forth; thus, they conclude that the idea of God is just a fairy tale or an illusion, and that those who choose to believe in Him are either brain-washed or simply uneducated. Though at times their reasoning may, on some level, make sense to many, when observed closely, one will find out that many holes exist within this view.

Think with me for a moment! How many of us humans have ever seen the nine planets that exist in our universe with our own eyes, yet, we believe that they do exist because we read and gather information from science books which were written by men, some of which date back to several decades or centuries. We put our complete trust in these writings believing the findings of others, the measurements they present to us about fossils, and much more of their scientific conclusions.

Is it not interesting how we believe many of these things even though we have not seen them personally? So then, if not seeing but believing things that are out of ones own reach would make one unintelligent, then would not those who deny God's existence because of their expressed faith in things they themselves have not had first hand encounters also fall into the very same category?

The universe has two great international preachers; these preachers are the heavens and the Earth! The heavens tells us of the great glory and power of the Almighty God, while the Earth tells of God's great works like His creation (Psalms 19:1-3) and (Romans 1:20). There is no place on the globe where their voices have not been heard or where their messages do not marvel men, yet unbelief is still prevalent. Have you ever taken the time to obverse the sky and become enthralled by all its decorative features: the stars, the moon, the sun, rainbows, and clouds?

These exist because of the working of God's own power, not because of what some refer to as the result of the "Big Bang". How about an examination of the world around us? Consider the mountains, the various species of, trees, animals, aquatic life, lakes, rivers, oceans, and of course man. All of these wonderful aspects of creation point in one clear direction; they point to God! He is their creator and He maintains them so that we can co-exist with them. Thus, even though Christians are deemed unintelligent for having faith in God, on the contrary, the Bible tells in (Psalms 14:1) that those who deny the existence of God are not wise, but are in reality fools.

There are many bodies of evidence that point to the existence of God, and there are literally millions of people who encountered this reality by way of personal experiences and by putting the claims of scriptures to the test for themselves. It is important for us to understand that it was never God's intention that He remained a being hidden from the knowledge of His creation. Thus, He has made it so that He can be personally known and experienced by any man or woman who desires to know Him.

God makes it rather difficult for anyone to remain agnostic uncommitted to believing in either the existence or non-existence of God). This is not the case in any other religious circle such as, Hinduism, Buddhism, Islam, Scientology, and so on. When you think about God, what first comes to your mind? What is your perspective of Him? Is He a common figure that you refer to as "the Man Upstairs", or "the Big Guy"? The portrait of God that is painted in the Bible is far different from those images.

THE EVOLUTION AND CREATION DEBATE

Within our educational circles, from kindergarten right up to university level, the idea that claims that God created human life is referred to as a myth. Most educators are quite comfortable teaching that humanity exists as the result of evolution. From a Christian perspective, how would you show that God is the Father of humanity and that humanity is not the result the process of evolution?

The Question of God Questions

1. Explain and discuss (Genesis 1:1)

2. Using (Genesis 1:2-26) as your base, discuss what the Bible teaches about creation

3. Explain and discuss (Jeremiah 10:11-16)

4. What three things does Jeremiah tell us about God and how does these attributes make the God of the Bible different from all other gods? (Jeremiah 10:10)

5. Explain and discuss (Psalms 19:1-3)

6. Why has God made the things that are invisible about Him known? (Romans 1:20)

7. How are people who deny the existence of God described? (Psalms 14:1)

8. Explain and discuss the four things that Paul tells us about God (1 Timothy 1:17)

9. In your own words, how can God be known?

CHAPTER SIX
The Problem of Sin

═══════════════════════════════════

DISCUSSION 3

At this point in our discussion, I will talk about sin and try to show where and how sin originated. I will begin by pointing out that the story describing how human begins became sinners is truly, in my estimation, the world's saddest story that has ever been told. This story details how God's perfectly created children, Adam and Eve, who were made to live forever and to enjoy endless companionship with God, became sinful people because of their disobedience to God's command.

Not only did their disobedience cause them to become sinners, but they also became servants and children of the Devil. Jesus points out this sad reality in His address to the Jews in (John 8:44) where, Jesus declared to them that they were children of the Devil and that their evil works were of the Devil "because the devil sinned from the beginning".

"In the beginning", we are told of how God created the first human in (Genesis 2:7) by molding him from the "dust of the ground" and then "breathing into his nostrils the breath of life" and from that moment on, man became "a living soul". Later in the book of Genesis, we are told that God took one of Adams ribs and formed Eve and placed them both in the Garden of Eden. There, while in the garden, the Bible tells us that God gave Adam a specific command.

(Genesis 2:15-17) relates this event where God told Adam that he could eat fruit from any tree in the garden except for the tree which contained the knowledge of good and evil. Adam was warned of what would happen if he should disobey God—he would "surely die". Regretfully, Adam did not heed God's warning and rather than seeking to please God, He decided to disobey God just like Satan did in the beginning.

This opens the door for me to introduce the topic of sin. The first point that I would like to make regarding sin is that all people in the world have sinned and have failed in some way or another to successfully live up to God's standard. Paul tells us of this in (Romans 3:23) where he states that "all have sinned and have come short of the glory of God". By this he shows that the issue of sin is a universal one and that no one except for Jesus Christ can say that they have no sin.

Not only does Paul point out that we are sinners, but John also tell us in (1 John 1:8), that if a person says that he has no sin, in reality he is simply deceiving himself and "the truth of God is not in him." In light of these facts, it is important that we understand just what sin really is, how God truly feels about it, and sin's many negative consequences.

Originally, when human beings decided to walk away from God, they began to commit great sins demonstrating just how depraved they had truly become after they fell. Paul tells us about these sins in (Romans 1:21) where he stated that when men knew God, they did not glorify Him as God. Paul also stated that they were not thankful to God for the many things that He had done for them. Now, these two serious acts of negligence took place in man's mind and also within their hearts and as a result paved the way for two negative consequences in their lives.

First, when men decided to turn away from God they became vain in their imaginations; and secondly, their foolish hearts became darkened by their sins. In other words, the quality of thinking that they had lost in their fall from God's standard, and the purity of heart that they once had were lost. It was then replaced with a darkness that came over their hearts and their actions revealed this darkness day by day.

I will now try to answer two main questions that people commonly ask. One, what is sin? And two, where did sin come from? For centuries, people have been asking these questions and the Bible is replete with practical answers. The Bible defines what sin is in (1 John 3:4) as being any transgression of God's holy laws. Another way to define sin is as an inward spiritual attitude of rebellion against God's will that is eventually expressed in outward actions of disobedience. The Ten Commandments recorded in (Exodus 20:1-17) also give us a clear picture of what God considers to be sinful acts.

These commandments are a list of religious and moral guidelines that outline how humans are supposed to behave in relation to God and in relation to their fellow man. For example, God says that we should not have or worship any graven image. Those who partake in idolatrous behaviors are showing that they are out of fellowship with God. Thus, this part of the commandment is God-ward. Another command is that humans should not lie. When we lie we can very well cause pain for those whom we lie against. This would forfeit the true purpose of the Ten Commandments which is to love God and to love man.

Anytime a person fails to obey any of God's words, that person is sinning even if he or she is not fully knowledgeable of what is written in God's Word. I find it very sad to note that there are people in the world who do not care very much about this universal epidemic of sin. Many of them live careless lives and do a good job of ignoring what the Word of God says about sin even if God's Word is right before their very faces. Some of these people also claim that there are no real or serious consequences for their wrongdoings, but how wrong they are! Again I will refer to Solomon to make my point clear. Solomon tells us in (Proverbs 16:25) that there is a way, perhaps a way of thinking that people have, but the end of that way will ultimately lead them to death.

The reality of this is that sin is a terrible thing. Sin is God's worst enemy if I can put it that way. I am confident in believing that sin was not a part of God's original plan when He created His angels, the universe, and human beings. I believe this because when God had completed designing all things, He stated in (Genesis 1:31) that everything was "very good". The earth was created with the intention of being a perfect place occupied by perfect people. So then, where did sin come from if God made all things well? Sin came into the universe when Lucifer, also called Satan, and his angels forsook their allegiance to God, and thus were cast out of Heaven. We are told about this situation in (Isaiah 14:12-15) and (Ezekiel 28:13- 19).

For the purpose of our discussion, I will look at what Isaiah said about Satan's actions and the consequences of his actions. Isaiah first points out that before Satan sinned; he was a "shining star". It is believed that Lucifer was the most beautiful angel in Heaven. He was loved very much by God and consequently he was placed second in command in Heaven.

As time went by, Lucifer decided that he no longer wanted to be second and therefore planned to overthrow God by desiring to set his throne above the stars of God. God would not tolerate that. Subsequently, he was expelled from Heaven and upon being expelled, he—Satan—devised a plan through which he hoped to get back at God by showing Him how angry he was. His plan would be tried on Adam and Eve hoping that if he succeeded, he might have them join him in his eternal home which we are told in (Matthew 25:41) is "everlasting fire." Satan knew that Adam and Eve were the greatest of God's creation and he was not pleased that they had taken the previous place he held with God in Heaven. His plan was to find ways that he might be able to successfully trick humans into disobeying God. Needless to say, Satan was successful in doing just that.

Not only was Satan able to deceive them both, but he would also cause their lives to be negatively impacted forever; and not only their lives, but our lives as well. Satan continues to work even in our time with the hope that he will be able to stop people from giving their lives to Jesus Christ, and he has a rather clever way of doing this. He causes people to be exposed to false teachings in addition to putting into their minds the desire to question God's Word by exposing them to theories and ideas such as evolution, which we mentioned before. Paul tells us in (2 Corinthians 4:3-4) that Satan is responsible for placing veils over the eyes of people with the sole purpose of preventing them from having open hearts that would allow them to receive the Gospel.

For centuries, Satan has taken people of all sorts of people as his captives, keeping them in an abyss of sin. He does this by lying and telling them that the life of sin that they live is really the way that human life was intended to be lived. Not only does he lie, but he also imposes several strongholds on their minds which make it hard for them to choose the right path, which is the path to becoming saved. These strongholds vary from mental bondage, to sexual bondage to religious bondage.

Satan's main wish is told to us by the Apostle John when he records in (John 10:10) that the thief (Satan) only comes to do three evil things and those are to steal, kill, and to destroy. Satan hates God and because of his hatred for God he equally hates God's children as well. His hatred for God is so strong that Peter tells us in (1 Peter 5:8) that we should be very careful and also that we should understand that we have an adversary who is the devil; one who walks around as if he were "a roaring lion" looking for people that would allow him to devour their lives. This goes to show us that the reality of Satan is a serious one and that it is imperative that we understand how he operates, as well as what his goals and desires are for human beings so that we might be able to live our lives in such a way that none of his evil schemes and plans can or will find their fulfillment in our destinies.

This now leads us to give an answer for where sin comes from and who is to be blamed for it. Is God to be blamed for sin? What about Satan; is he to be totally blamed? The truth is this: Satan is responsible for sin's entrance in the universe; however, Adam is the one who is held responsible for introducing sin to the human race. Paul makes this point very clear in (Romans 5:12). It should be clear to us all that rebellion is an act that God truly hates and one that He will never, ever tolerate. God did not tolerate rebellion when it was detected in Satan, nor did he tolerate it in Adam and Eve; you and I are no different because God is no respecter of persons.

THE EFFECTS OF SIN

In this second part of our discussion about sin, I will talk about the effects of sin. Sin's effects are very powerful and they are plentiful. Sin is followed by three main consequences: first, spiritual death which causes a person to be alienated from God; and secondly, physical death where humans will one day return to the earth that they originally came from. These two are followed by the most serious consequence which is eternal death. Those who did not obey God's Word will live apart from God in eternal punishment in the lake of fire.

All of these consequences of sin are a clear indication that God sincerely hates sin. But do we really know why He hates sin so much? God hates sin because sin makes it difficult for Him to enjoy unbroken fellowship with the people whom He loves so dearly. Isaiah tells us of this in (Isaiah 59:1-2) where he states that the sins of people have separated them from God, and thus, blocks their ability to communicate with God freely.

Before Adam and Eve's rebellion, they had no knowledge of sin or of sin's cruel effects; but the moment that they disobeyed God by eating from the tree, they instantly became sinful people. The truth is that when Adam first sinned, all human beings existed in his loins; and thus, all people became sinners even before their birth! This leads me to understand that human beings are not sinners because they have sinned at various times during their lives, but we were born that way, in a state of sin. Because of this, which I will discuss later on in this book, all people have a need to be born-again (John 3:3-5). In the same manner in which an unborn baby is able to contract a disease from its parents, all of humanity has contracted the disease of sin from Adam, their first father. David, in (Psalm 51:5), tells us that we are all born into sin.

He says that he was born a sinner; therefore, Adam and Eve's sin went way beyond their act of disobedience; it changed their entire genetic structure. Furthermore, they were automatically born under Satan's rule which Paul points out in (Romans 6:16), letting us know that anything or anyone that we yield ourselves to, we become slaves to. This was very true for Adam and Eve.

So now, all can clearly see that it was not the day that we might have first stolen the "cookie from the cookie jar" that we first became sinners; our fate was sealed long before that. Sin is in all of our genes and only Jesus Christ can remove it.

WHAT HAPPENED TO ALL MY SINS?

When people repent of their sins and accept Jesus Christ into their hearts, what really happens to all of their past sins? Are their sins really forgiven? I have found in my experience of working with various people that many of them are not always sure that their many sins are forgiven and that they will never be used against them in the future. David was a person who had committed many sins during his lifetime. One day, he came to a conclusion and said in (Psalms 103:8-14) that God has removed all of his sins from him as far as the east is from the west. This is a very powerful truth for us to understand! The beauty of this passage is that the east and the west never meet in the way that the north and south poles do; therefore, I believe that it is fair for me to say that we have been completely separated from our past sins when we ask for God's forgiveness.

It is important for you to know that God is not like man and that He does not lie (Numbers 23:19). God does not promise one thing but deliver another. You can trust in His every word. Jesus Christ has taken your sins and has put them in a place where they have no more power to control any aspect of your life. They have all been cast into the sea of forgetfulness.

For our conversation regarding what happens to a person's sin when they come to Jesus for forgiveness, I would also consider (Isaiah 43:25), where God says that it is He that blots out the transgressions of humankind, and in the same breath He states that He will remember their sins no more. Here is something to think about for a moment: if God is all-knowing and nothing is able to escape His eyes; how is it then possible for Him to forget our sins? Does God remember them but just does not allow them to bother Him? No, that is not the case. He means just what He said: He remembers them no more. As humans, this is very difficult for us to understand.

If someone was to hurt you in any way, very often you might say that you will forgive that person, but you cannot forget what they have done. So we may hold a grudge against that person for what they have done to us, or even to others whom we love or are connected to. But this is not the case with God. When He forgives, He forgets; amazing, isn't it! So, it does not matter what kinds of sins were manifested in your life, whether your sins were anger, lying, stealing, worrying, adultery, homosexuality, or any other kind. The sins of sinners are placed under the blood of Jesus Christ.

WHO IS SATAN AND WHAT ROLE DOES HE REALLY PLAY IN THE WORLD?

A lot of attention is generally placed on God, but many people do not think about the Devil or the role that he plays in the things that happen in the world. Describe what the Bible has to say about Satan and also what role Satan plays within societies all over the world.

The Problem of Sin Questions

1. What is the Bible's definition of sin (1 John 3:4)

2. What does Paul tell us about all of humanity? (Romans 3:23)

3. Explain and discuss (John 8:44)

4. Explain and discuss (Genesis 2:15-17)

5. What are we told about people who might say that they are not sinners? (1 John 1:8)

6. What two sins did humans commit when they decided to turn away from God? (Romans 1:21)

7. List each of the sins mentioned in (Exodus 20:1-17) and show how they hurt both God and men

8. Explain and discuss (Proverbs 16:25)

9. What are some things that people do that might lead them down a path of destruction?

10. Explain and discuss (Genesis 1:31)

11. What does (Isaiah 14:12-15) revel about Satan?

12. What three statements did Satan make that caused him to be expelled from heaven?

13. What is one of Satan's key tools for keeping humans in darkness? (2 Corinthians 4:4)

14. Explain and discuss (John 10:10)

15. Explain and discuss (1 Peter 5:8)

16. Who is responsible for introducing sin to the human race? (Romans 5:12)

17. Why is sin such a huge deal to God? (Isaiah 59:1-2)

18. Explain and discuss (Psalm 51:5)

19. What does Paul tell us is the final payment for sin? (Romans 6:23)

20. Explain and discuss (Psalms 103:12)

21. What do we learn about God? (Numbers 23:19)

22. Explain and discuss (Isaiah 43:25)

CHAPTER SEVEN
Who is Jesus Christ?

═══════════════════════════

DISCUSSION 4

Who, in reality, is Jesus Christ and what did He say about himself in the Bible? I will begin by pointing out a story that was told in the book of Matthew. One day while Jesus conversed with His disciples, He asked them what people in the streets were saying about Him. His disciples replied and said that some people were saying that He was John the Baptist; some said that He was Elijah, and others said that perhaps he was Jeremiah or one of the other prophets. By this, it is clear that Jesus' identity was as hot of a topic as it is today. As Jesus' conversation continued, He then posed that same question to His disciples asking them who they thought He was. We can find this story in (Matthew 16:13-20).

From the midst of the disciples, Peter spoke up and gave an outstanding revelation regarding Jesus' identity. He said, "You are the Son of the living God". This was a powerful revelation that Peter made because by stating that Jesus was the Son of God that implied He was unlike any other human being.

After Peter had made this outstanding confession, Jesus made him a unique promise. Jesus told Peter first that his name would be changed, and not only that; but that He would build His Church on Peter's confession of Him. In other words, what Jesus wanted Peter and all others to understand is that His Church is built on the fact that He is the "Son of God" and that without conforming to this knowledge, a person cannot claim to be a part of the Church.

JESUS IS THE SAVIOUR OF ALL

Jesus Christ is the Savior of humanity! When Jesus walked the earth two thousand years ago, His paramount goal was to bring hope and salvation to all. Jesus knew very well that without Him, no man or woman could ever be saved from Satan and Satan's lies. This truth is made clear in (Luke 19:10) where we are told that Jesus came into the world to look for and to save individuals who were lost, and this includes everyone. Jesus is not *a* savior, meaning that there are others who are capable for offering salvation as well, but He is the only Savior.

He is the only one who is able to deliver humanity from the wrath of sin. Many people seem to believe that they can choose who or what they will go to for their salvation. Some people choose to tell their sins to a priest while others pray to saints and to Mary while others try to obtain salvation through their own willpower.

But the Bible is clear that coming to Jesus is the only way a person can receive salvation because Jesus in the only way to God. John tells us of this in (John 14:6) where Jesus declared that He was "the way the truth and the life" and that no person would be able to come to the Father without going through Him.

JESUS IS GOD!

Unlike Buddha, Mohammed and other religious figures, Jesus was not just an ordinary man; He was the God-man, meaning that He was fully God and at the same time He was fully man. In (John 1:1), we are told that "in the beginning" the Word existed, and that "the Word was God". In (verse 2), we are told that all things were made by the Word and that without Him, nothing was made. John continues to reveal that "the Word became flesh" (John 1:14) and dwelled among those who lived at that time. Cleary we can conclude that John was speaking in regard to Jesus Christ and His entrance into Earth. God took on human flesh, for the very first time in history, and appeared on earth as Jesus the one who would save humans from their sin as we are told in (Matthew 1:21). Now in order for God who is a Spirit (John 4:24) to establish and offer His plan of salvation, He needed a body through which he would lay down His life on the cross (Hebrews 10:5), and shed His blood which would eventually wash away the sins of mankind (Hebrews 9:22).

This would not be a truth that would be difficult to believe for those who know and understand that God is all-powerful and sovereign, meaning that He can do anything that He wants to do whenever He chooses to. He can be a pillar of cloud during the day for the children of Israel, while a pillar of fire during night (Numbers 14:14). When Moses had his first real encounter with God, in which he was commissioned by God to lead the children of Israel out of slavery into freedom, he asked for God what His name was (Exodus 3:13-14). Moses wanted to be able to tell all those whom he would lead the name of the God he was asked to represent. He was then commanded to tell all the people that he was sent by "I am that I am".

This is a rather unique revelation that Moses received. In a nutshell, God wanted Moses and all others to know that He would not be limited; He was whatever He needed to be at any given time. If what the children of Israel needed was salvation from their enemies, then God would be their salvation. If perhaps they needed someone who would provide for them, then He would be their provider and so forth. He would not be put into a box. Many people do not believe in Jesus and they deny His claims of being God. Two examples of this are found in (John 8:56-59) and (John 10:30-33). In both of these passages, Jesus makes claims for which He received a negative response from His audiences.

First, He claimed that He was older than Abraham, the father of the Jewish nation; secondly, He claimed that He and God were one. Both times His listeners, mostly Jews, wanted to stone Him. Jesus in the latter scripture passage asked His listeners why they wanted to stone Him, and they confessed that their motivation was based on the fact that by saying that He and God were one, He was making Himself God. But indeed, Jesus is God.

In another situation Jesus, as He would regularly do, spoke about His Father. He was asked by Philip just who His Father was. Philip was sure that if Jesus could show Him the Father, he would be satisfied (John 14:7-9). Jesus responded to Philip almost in shock. He asked Philip, "How can I be with you for such a long time and you do not know who I am." From Jesus' response to Philip, no honest person could deny that Jesus did not claim to be God in the Bible. Finally, though there are many other passages that teach this wonderful truth of Jesus being God, (John 20:28) tells us of Thomas' revelation after Christ's resurrection when he responded to Jesus by saying "my Lord and my God".

Upon hearing this proclamation Jesus did not correct Thomas's statement. Paul also reveals that without any doubt, "God was manifested" into flesh, and then once His work was finished here on earth, He was taken back up "into glory" (1 Timothy 3:16). This reference to God actually points to Jesus because in (Acts 1:11) we see Jesus' ascension into Heaven after He had finished His assignment on Earth.

There will come a day when all of humanity will come to recognize just who Jesus really is, and they will all at that time bow their knees and confess His Lordship. If we will all be compelled to do this at the very mention of His name on that day (Philippians 2:9-11), then why not do it now? We are all given the chance to choose. We can choose to confess Jesus' Lordship now or later in the judgment hall. Compare this with (Isaiah 45:23) where the same words are used in reference to the God of the Old Testament. These passages both reveal that Jesus was not only man, but that He was God.

WHY DID JESUS REALLY DIE?

What an amazing truth that human life was exchanged for human life when Jesus died on Calvary. What are the odds that anyone would die for another person, especially if that person was a bad person? This is what Jesus did as we are clearly told by Paul in (Romans 5:7-8) where Paul says that not only would one find it hard to die for a righteous person but that this Jesus died for humans even while they were still sinners.

Our history books are filled with the lives, accomplishments, and deaths of many famous people. Some of these people were prominent men and women from various parts of the world. Consider for a moment if you will: Abraham Lincoln, John A. McDonald, Mohammed, Martin Luther King, Jr., and Mother Teresa just to name a few. Their deaths were mourned by thousands because of the amazing work they did while on earth. When one looks at the honor and esteem bestowed on these great men and women, however, the amazing truth is underlined that none of these individuals' deaths can or should be viewed in the same light as the death of Jesus Christ.

But why is Christ's death so completely different from the deaths of others? First, Jesus was a sinless man who was sent to earth by His Father to make atonement for the sins of all human beings. He did not inherit the sinful nature that every other human being received at birth. However, all of the other men and woman mentioned before, though they played significant roles in history, had a sin problem that they themselves were unable to eliminate.

Secondly, the Islamic prophet, Mohammed, is still in the grave and the others are there as well; but Jesus Christ rose from the dead on the third day, gaining power over Satan and the world of darkness! We are told of the resurrection of Jesus Christ from the dead in many places in the Bible. Consider what Paul says in (1 Corinthians 15:1-4). The final words of Christ while He was on the cross were powerful words. He looked into the heavens and said aloud the fateful words, "It is finished" (John 19:30). What was Jesus referring to when He said this? I believe that He was referring to the fact that the price that was required to defeat the power of sin was paid for in full when He died. Also the words, "It is finished" points out that Satan's power would be broken once men and women chose to receive salvation.

The death of Jesus was not an afterthought because the Bible says in (Revelation 13:8) that Jesus was slain before the foundation of the earth. In actuality, Jesus was not physically slain until the New Testament period which quite obviously was ushered in a very long while after the creation of the earth. However, because God knows all things even before they happen, in His mind and plan, Jesus was slain even before men sinned. This does not mean that God planned for man to sin; that would be far from the truth. But His fore-knowledge caused Him to see what would take place in the lives of all people and He provided a way for their rescue.

Why did Jesus Christ really have to die, and more specifically, why did He have to die in the manner which He did? Was it because He was a madman as some believe? No! Does Jesus' death really have a clear and life-changing meaning for humanity? Yes! As was discussed before, God created mankind with the intention of enjoying endless fellowship with His creation; but instead, the people whom He loved so dearly were tricked and taken captive by Satan. Because of this, they were unable to enjoy life in the manner that God had intended for them to and God had to do something drastic; something so drastic that it would daze and confuse the dark world and create an escape for the precious children.

Paul tells us in (Galatians 4:4-5) that in the fullness of time, God executed His plan of action. God's plan to rescue and recover mankind would entail the laying down of the life of His only Son on the cross. This is seen throughout many passages in the Bible, from the Old Testament to the New Testament. In the book of Isaiah, we are told about the death that Jesus Christ would experience through the form of a cruel type of crucifixion (Isaiah 53:1-12). Within these verses, we are told that there would come a time during the life of Jesus Christ that He would be so badly beaten that those who saw Him would see no beauty in Him. Also, Isaiah tells us further that He would be despised and rejected by mankind, and that He would become a man of sorrow, one acquainted with extreme grief. Jesus Christ encountered all of this in order that He would be able to bear our grief and to carry our sorrows.

Moreover, but Jesus would be wounded for the transgressions of human beings and also be bruised for their iniquities. So if we were to truly attempt to determine the real purpose or cause for the death of Jesus Christ, we would have to conclude that the cause for Jesus' death was the sins of humanity. Every lie that we have told during our lives, every act of sexual immorality, or any other sin we have committed are what drove Jesus Christ to the cross to die in our stead.

It would not be until the New Testament dispensation that we would see the fulfillment of what Isaiah the prophet foretold regarding the crucifixion of Jesus. All four of the Gospel writers— Matthew, Mark, Luke, and John—give us separate accounts of the death of Jesus Christ and the many atrocities that He encountered in order to atone for the sins of humanity.

At this point, I would like to turn our focus to the account of Jesus' death that was presented by Matthew. Matthew describes how Christ was betrayed by Judas and also how He was mocked and crucified for His claims of being the Son of God (Matthew 27).

From the onset, Jesus' mission was to ensure that Satan's grip on humanity would be loosened, and Jesus did just that when He died on the cross! He both destroyed the works of the Devil and set free the captives Satan had held bound for thousands of years. This is shown in (1 John 3:8) and (Colossians 1:12-14). As a result of Jesus' death and His resurrection, as many people who would believe Jesus' work that was done on the cross and accept it by obeying His plan for salvation, would in return be saved from Satan and from Satan's ultimate will for their lives.

UNCONDITIONAL LOVE

One of God's most salient attributes is His love. God is love! (1 John 4:8). This statement doesn't simply mean that God has the ability to love; this truth goes much further than that. What it is saying is that God cannot be separated from love, just as love cannot be separated from God. Therefore, to understand love is to understand God. As a result of this truth, all of God's dealings with humanity stem from His Love for them. God is madly in love with humanity, and His love for humanity is unconditional. This means that no matter what condition peoples' lives may be in, or whatever acts they will have committed at various times in their lives, God's love for them always remains strong. We are told of this in (Jeremiah 31:3) where God says that He loves his people with an everlasting love.

It was as a direct result of God's love that He was able to provide salvation through the death of Jesus Christ. We are also told of God's love in (John 3:16). Here, we are given an illustration of the world's greatest love story. We are told that because of God's intense love for humanity, he offered the life of His only Son with the intention of bringing salvation to all. God's love towards humanity does not stem from any good that humanity has done. We are told by Paul in (Romans 5:8) that "while we were still sinners," Jesus Christ died for us. He did not wait for us to become perfect before He gave His precious life; but rather, He offered His life knowing that it was impossible for us to become perfect or good through our own efforts.

John tells us about the magnitude of God's love again in (1 John 3:1) where he says, "Behold, what manner of love the Father has bestowed upon us." "This wonderful gesture of love so fascinated John that he was compelled to direct his readers to "behold what manner of love". He understood that Jesus' sacrifice was a true and genuine act of unusual love. Never had any other person shown such a quantity and quality of love in the history of the human experience as God did by offering His Son. Because of this act, Paul also tells us in (Ephesians 2:8) that an individual is saved through faith; they are not saved by their own efforts because salvation is a gift from God.

JESUS IS THE ONLY WAY
TO SALVATION

I f Jesus is the only way to God, where does that leave other religions?

Please take the time needed and fill in an answer for each of the following questions below by both reading them in your Bibles and also looking back into the chapter for the correct answers. It is recommended that you use your answers to these questions to help you when you teach your own personal Bible Studies.

Who is Jesus Christ? Questions

1. What was Jesus' question to His disciples? (Matthew 16:13-20)

2. What response was He given to His question?

3. What was Peter's confession and why was that important?

4. What was Jesus' purpose for coming into the earth? (Luke 19:10)

5. What three things did Jesus claim? (John 14:6)

6. What problem do these three claims pose for other religions and religious leaders?

7. Explain and discuss (John 1:1-2)

8. Explain and discuss (John 1:14)

9. What truth do we learn about God? (John 4:24)

10. What did Jesus need in order for Him to die on the cross (Hebrews 10:5)

11. Explain and discuss (Hebrews 9:22)

12. Explain and discuss (John 8:56-59)

13. What did Jesus mean when He stated that He was before

Abraham?

14. What did Jesus reveal? (John 10:30)

15. Why did the Jews desire to stone Jesus (John 10:30-33)

16. Who did Philip desire to know? (John 14:8)

17. Explain and discuss Jesus' response (John 14:9)

18. What did Thomas refer to Jesus as and why is this important? (John 20:28)

19. Explain and discuss (1 Timothy 3:16). Compare this with (Acts 1:11)

20. When God exalted Jesus what did He give Him? (Philippians 2:9)

21. Explain and discuss (Philippians 2:10-11). Compare this with (Isaiah 45:23)

22. When did God show His love toward humans? (Romans 5:8)

23. What did Jesus mean when He said "it is finished"? (John 19:30)

24. Explain and discuss (Revelation 13:8)

25. According to Paul when did God send Jesus into the earth and why did He send His Son? (Galatians 4:4-5)

26. Explains and discuss (Isaiah 53:1-12)

27. Explain and discuss (1 John 3:8) and (Colossians 1:12-14)

28. What do we learn about God? (1 John 4:8)

29. What does Jeremiah say about God's love? (Jeremiah 31:3)

30. Explain and discuss (John 3:16)

31. Explain and discuss (1 John 3:1)

CHAPTER EIGHT
The Plan for Salvation

DISCUSSION 5

I have now arrived at the fourth part of our discussion where I will discuss the subject of salvation. This subject is of great significance because all people in the world need to be saved. Did you know that the first disease to ever be diagnosed in humans still exists today? This catastrophic disease is none other than sin which, according to (Romans 3:23), is a universal crisis. Sin was first contracted and spread to all of humanity by Adam and Eve? What a terrible scenario!

Because of this horrible disease, all people will one day experience death and none of us will ever be able to escape it, no matter how hard we may try.

Before I go on, I will try to answer two questions that are often asked: First, why is this plan for salvation essential and why do men and women need to come to Jesus Christ for their salvation? And secondly, can a person be saved by employing their own efforts?

The plan of salvation is vital because without it, all men and women would have no chance of eternal life with Jesus. Consequently, so many churches, religions, and doctrines? In (Ephesians 4:5), we are told that there is only one Lord, one faith, and one baptism. This means that if there are a million different beliefs about what is takes for a person to be saved, only one can be right because God has established only one way for all to participate in the gift of eternal life. God has a single plan for salvation and this plan is identical for all believers. So how can we know which way is true? We can only know which presentation of salvation is the truth by looking into the Bible and seeing what it teaches.

There are many parts of the Bible which at first can be somewhat difficult to understand. Perhaps these parts are difficult because when they were written, they were written to people of a different culture than are familiar with today. Also, there are some difficulties that arise when one tries to understand some of the prophecies in parts of the Old Testament or even in the Book of Revelation. Nonetheless, passages that deal with God's plan for salvation do not need any interpretation at all because they are straightforward and they can be taken at face value.

As a result of this, each person is responsible for making sure that he or she knows the truth about how they are supposed to be saved and that they act upon that truth once they discover it in the Bible. The Bible gives a clear and simple outline for how a person is to be saved and, consequently, outside of obeying these simple steps of faith, men and women cannot enter into the Kingdom of God that Jesus talks about in (John 3:1-5). This passage gives a glimpse of the biblical outline of the message and truths regarding salvation, namely: faith, repentance, water baptism, and the baptism of the Holy Spirit.

STEP I

Faith

According to (Hebrews 11:6), before a person can confess Jesus Christ and make Him Lord of their hearts, they must express faith in God. Faith is important because without it no person can ever truly please God. Faith is the first step in the process of salvation. But what is faith? Faith is simply believing and then acting upon what is believed! Because faith is so important, it is necessary for us to discuss how a person obtains faith. We are told how by Paul in (Romans 10:17) that faith will come when the Word of Christ is talked about and heard. But faith in God alone cannot save a person. A person's faith in God, if they really have faith that is, will always lead them to act upon what they believe about God and also to be obedient to the Word of God.

Some people tend to believe that because they hold on to the belief that Jesus is real and that He died and rose again from the dead for their sins, they are saved; but this is not the case. James tells us about faith and also about the works that faith will produce in (James 2:14-17). In short, James questions what the purpose is of someone saying that he or she believes but doesn't show works to prove that belief. James asks, "Can faith alone save?" Finally, James tells us that if we only have faith without having works; all that is truly demonstrated that really shows is that our faith is dead (verse 17). Talk is cheap, and just verbalizing one's confession about Jesus Christ does not mean that a person really has faith, because true faith only comes to life when we act upon what the Word of God asks us to do.

only Jesus Christ can save a person from their sins and give them life again. God never does anything without planning it out from start to finish; therefore, He never encounters surprises. When the first two people sinned in the Garden of Eden, they were not left without hope; God had begun His rescue plan known as salvation. Salvation is the act of God converting and saving humanity from the final consequence of sin–eternal death–through the sacrifice of Jesus Christ on the cross.

The word *conversion* means to change or to transform something into something else. Through the process of salvation a person takes on a new nature and becomes "a new creation" as we are told of by Paul in (2 Corinthians 5:17) where says that if any man is in Jesus Christ he is "a new creation". Every single person who has ever been born into this world, whether they know it or not is in need of Salvation because all of us have sinned against God in countless ways. When God began putting His plan together, He took the time to ensure that it would include all humans who wanted to be saved. Therefore, whosoever wants to be saved, according to (Revelation 22:17), can be saved because Jesus loves us all and has died for us all. However, despite God's care in putting together His plan for salvation, many people over the past two thousand years have tried to pervert it by creating their own ideas around it. In one aspect, some have made the process of salvation out to be far too complicated, while in other respects, some have simply watered it down making it a thing of no value.

From time to time, when we pick up a religious tract at a Laundromat or bus stop, or when we simply turn on the television, we will be exposed to a great deal of ideas and notions regarding how a person is to apply God's designed plan for salvation. Some people say that all one needs to do to be born again (saved) is to simply be a good person, while others believe that all one needs to do is to say the "sinner's prayer". These views, however, are not what the Bible teaches about God's plan of salvation as you will come to understand upon searching the Bible. You will also discover that doing things God's way is of vital importance, especially when it pertains to the issue of salvation.

The Bible tells us clearly that the time will come when people will not endure sound teachings, but instead, they will turn a deaf ear to the truth and look for teachers who will tell them what they want to hear even if what they are being told is not the truth (2 Timothy 4:3-4). This leads us to ask an important question: what really is the truth? This question has been at the center of philosophical debates for some time now. Yet, there is only one answer to this question: truth is the Word of God. God's Word is the only source of truth that we have. Anything we believe that falls outside the realm of God's Word is subject to error, and anything that we might believe that is contrary to His Word is a lie. How a person might think or perhaps even feel is irrelevant to the truth. The truth will remain the truth no matter who may or may not believe it.

In the book of (Romans 3:3-4), Paul asks an important question: what if some people do not believe the Word of God; will their lack of faith make God's Word ineffective? The answer to this question is no! Paul concluded by saying "let God be true" and all those who challenge Him liars. Therefore, even if every person in the world were to choose to believe a lie, God's Word would still stand true. Peter also agrees with this fact as evidenced by his statement in (1 Peter 1:24-25) where says that all humans are like grass and that their glory will one day fade away just as flowers do. But as for the Word of God it will never fade way; it will endure forever.

Well, since there is only one source of truth, then why are there

Repentance of Sins

After a person has expressed faith in God, that individual is in need of faith (in order) to take the next step." This next step is the act of repentance as stated in (Luke 24:46-47). There is no man or woman who is above repentance because, as stated before, all people have sinned in some way or another and have fallen short of God's expectation of them. Consequently, repentance is vital to receiving Jesus Christ into one's life. But what exactly is repentance?

To sum it up, repentance is not just feeling sorrowful, or crying, or even feeling bad. Rather, repentance takes place when a man or woman takes clear action to turn away from sin. When sinners repent, they must first acknowledge that they are sinners, and once they have come to this understanding, they need to develop a change of mind and remorse for the sins that they have committed throughout their lives, no matter how great or small they might consider their sins to be.

Many people believe because they have shed tears about their sins that perhaps that act constitutes repentance. But the Bible says in (2 Corinthians 7:10) that godly sorrow will lead a person to repentance unto salvation. Consequently, if one's repentance does not lead one to God, then that repentance is not real. If someone was asked to summarize the message of John the Baptist, they could do so by using one word and that word is *repent*.

From the beginning of John's and even Jesus' teachings, they called people to repent and to make their lives right with God. In (Luke 3:8), John tells the people who came to him that they needed first of all to repent, and also to prove that their repentance was sincere by showing fruits. John was not talking about physical fruits, but rather evident actions that were much more than mere verbal confessions and expressions of remorse.

The picture of repentance that is depicted in the Bible is that of a person turning away from a sinful way of living, and turning toward God pledging to live a life dedicated to doing things His way from that point onward. God promises in (1 John 1:9) that He will forgive those who come to Him of all their sins no matter how monstrous those sins may seem.

Finally, let us understand that there is a clear contrast between the confession of sins and the actual act of repentance. With confession, a person verbally makes their sinful acts known to God, but with repentance that person stops willfully sinning and aims towards living a life of righteousness. So the act of repentance truly prepares a person to receive Jesus into their hearts. One cannot continue to sin and at the same time please God. In (Romans 6:1), Paul asked a practical question that we too should ask. He asked if we should continue sinning so that God's grace could abound. His answer to this was a resounding, no!

In another passage (1 Corinthians 6:9-10), Paul makes it clear that those who are sinful will not make it into the kingdom of God. However, if a person chooses to repent from a sinful way of living, at the exact point in which that person repents, God will forgive those sins and at that instantly begin to transform that individual into a completely new person. Based on this truth, there is no reason for believers to run away from God when they have sinned, feeling that what they might have done in their lives against God is too bad, and that God cannot forgive them. If they humble themselves and make right with God, He will wash them and accept them that at the very moment they pray and ask for His forgiveness. He will also, as Paul said in (Romans 5:1), justify them making it just like they had not sinned at all.

STEP 3

Water Baptism

Repentance leads us to another essential step in God's plan in preparing humans to have His Spirit dwell within their hearts. We are told more about this plan of salvation in (Acts 2:38). This is the third step on the road to salvation—the command to be baptized in water in the name of Jesus Christ. When Jesus died on the cross, He shed His blood to remove our sin but that blood is not instantaneously applied to our lives. We can only access Jesus' cleansing blood by calling on His name in baptism.

What exactly does *baptism* mean? Briefly, baptism means to be dipped or to be immersed in something insomuch that whatever is dipped becomes completely saturated. Baptism is an important act of obedience and faith through which an individual re-enacts the death, burial, and resurrection of Jesus Christ. This act of faith is accomplished once a person who believes in the message of salvation is completely immersed in water in the name of Jesus (Romans 6:3-4) explains this.

Water baptism does not cleanse a person physically, but rather baptism cleanses a person spiritually. We find this truth discussed in (1 Peter 3:21) where Peter states that through the act of baptism, a person will come to have a "good conscience toward God". It is needful for us to make it clear that the only way for an individual to have a "good conscience toward God" is for that person to deal with their issue of sin.

The act of baptism declares that a person's sins have been washed away. This was revealed in (Acts 22:16) where Paul, after he had received his sight, asked them what they were waiting for and instructed them to go and wash away their sins by being baptized and by calling Jesus' name. From these and other passages, we can see that water baptism in not optional; it is a commandment (Acts 10:48), and it is vital for receiving the work of atonement that Jesus completed when He died on the cross.

On the day of Pentecost while the Apostle Peter was preaching in (Acts 2:37) to a crowd of more than three thousand, he was asked a very important question! He was asked what a person should do after they were told about Jesus' love for them as demonstrated by His death on the cross. Peter responded without hesitation to that question. He told the listeners in the crowd that they needed to repent and be baptized in the name of Jesus Christ in order to remove their sins. He also told them they needed to receive the baptism of the Holy Spirit (Acts 2:38).

Peter was clear in his answer! He did not tell his listeners that all they needed to do was pray a prayer, or simply believe that Jesus died and rose again from the dead, or even to attend Church regularly, though those things are all important. What Peter told this group is still true for the man or woman asking the "how to be saved" question today! They must believe, repent, and be water baptized.

Jesus Christ, in His teachings and preaching was very clear about the importance of baptism as well. He even linked the act of baptism to a person's salvation. He taught in (Mark 16:16) that those who believe and are baptized would be saved. In addition to this, we are told in (Galatians 3:27) that those who have been baptized into Christ have, in essence, put on Christ. This passage leads one to ask how someone can claim to be saved if they have not put on Christ. If Christ is put on through baptism, one can only agree that baptism is essential. Many in the religious world teach that baptism comes after a person has been saved. But in light of the above passage and the previous passage as well, this teaching cannot be considered as true.

Finally, not only is it of vital importance that all persons who believe in Jesus Christ be baptized, but it is also vital that their baptism be performed only in the name of Jesus. When Jesus gave His disciples the "Great Commission" in (Matthew 28:19), He told them that they should go and preach the Gospel in all parts of the earth. He commanded them to baptize people and that they should do so in the name of Father, and of the Son, and of the Holy Spirit. Many have used this passage to perform baptisms that exclude the name of Jesus. One might ask if this really matters.

The truth is that without calling on the name of Jesus in baptism, there is no remission of sins. Jesus clearly gave His disciples the command to baptize individuals using His name. Notice that when Jesus told His followers to baptize people in the name, that the word name is singular, not plural. Most of us understand that the terms Father, Son and Spirit are not names but rather titles. I have a father but Father is not my dad's name; you might be a son or a daughter but Son or Daughter is not your name; and God is a Holy Spirit but Holy Spirit is not His name.

God is so particular about His name being used, that in (Acts 4:10-12) we are told that the name of Jesus is the only name through which a person can be saved. Therefore, we can be sure that salvation only comes in the name of Jesus. Also, in (Philippians 2:9), we are told again about the power that resides in the name of Jesus. Paul says that God has highly exalted Jesus, and by doing so, He gave Jesus a name that is above every other name and at the name of Jesus every knee will bow. The knees of those in Heaven will bow at the name of Jesus; the knees of those upon the Earth will also bow, as well as the knees of those that are under the earth.

So what is the name of the Father? What is the name of the Son? And what is the name of the Holy Spirit which Jesus speaks about? There are many passages that give an answer to each of these questions. Not many people would challenge the fact that the name of the Son is Jesus. We are told this in (Matthew 1:21) where an angel tells Joseph that Mary would have a child and that the child's name would be called Jesus.

In (Hebrews 1:4), Paul tells us just how Jesus received His name: Paul sated that He received His name "by inheritance." That would mean that the name of Jesus received was handed down to Him by His father. Therefore, it can be concluded that the name of the Father is Jesus. Also, in (Isaiah 9:6), we are told again about Jesus' birth. The prophet declares, "Unto us a child is born." This he said in reference to Jesus; then He went on to say, "Unto us a son is given". But he did not stop there, because we are also told that the name of this child would be called: "Wonderful, Counselor, Mighty God", and "Everlasting Father" and even the "Prince of Peace". Let us notice that Isaiah considers Jesus to be the "mighty God" and the "everlasting Father".

Likewise, the name of the Holy Spirit is Jesus as (John 14:16-18 and 26). Here, Jesus talks about Him sending the comforter who He tells us is the Holy Spirit. Now let's take a closer look at just how I have come to say along with others that Jesus is the Holy Spirit. Jesus said that He would not leave His disciples comfortless; rather, He would come to them again. Just how would Jesus do that? Well He would come to them as the comforter the (Holy Spirit). In (John 14:18) Jesus said that He will ask the Father to send the comforter in His name, and again in (John 15:26) He says that He will send the comforter from the Father, and also in (John 16:7) He makes the same statement. Not only would Jesus be responsible for sending the comforter, but He would be that very same comforter as well.

For this reason all those who were baptized in the book of Acts were baptized exclusively in the name of the Lord Jesus because they understood that when Jesus commanded baptism for all people in the name of the Father, and of the Son, and of the Holy Ghost, that He intended for them to obey by using the name of the Father, and of the Son, and of the Holy Ghost. Jesus was not expecting that He would be repeated; He was expecting to be obeyed. Many other passages throughout the Bible also teach this truth. Consider (Acts 10:47-48) and (19:1-5) as examples of this truth.

The Baptism of the Holy Spirit

Receiving the baptism of the Holy Spirit is the next step in the process of salvation and it is as equally important as all the other steps mentioned before. The baptism of the Holy Spirit is a supernatural experience sent by Jesus Christ into the hearts of men and women who surrender their lives to Him. In a word, the Holy Spirit is God living in human beings. The Bible has many things to say about the Holy Spirit and how it would be received by Jesus' followers.

Many people have asked if the baptism of the Holy Spirit is for everyone. The correct response to this question is, yes; it is God's intention that all human beings experience the baptism of the Holy Spirit. We are told this in (Joel 2:28) and also in (Acts 2:39). Joel promised that in the last days, God would pour out His Spirit upon all flesh. This prophecy was later fulfilled in the book of (Acts 2:1-4) where all those who waited for Jesus' promise were filled with the Holy Spirit.

A person who might be a believer in Jesus and may even attend church regularly, will not be able to enter God's kingdom of Heaven when they die or be caught up to meet the Creator when the rapture (this is when Christ will come for take away the church, both those who have died as believers and those Christians who are alive and are living for Him) this is seen in (1 Thessalonians 4:15-17). In order for a person to enter into Heaven, he or she *must* be born-again. This is seen in (John 3:3-8) where Jesus makes it clear that men and women alike need to be born of "water and of the spirit".

When diners sit down in a restaurant, they are usually given a choice regarding what they would like to eat on that particular visit. Sometimes they are asked to choose between lobster, crab, chicken, steak, water, soda, juice, or a virgin Pina Colada. They can even have a lemon on the side if they so choose. But receiving the baptism of the Holy Spirit is not an optional dish or beverage to choose from. It is a must as Jesus and others in the Bible teach (Romans 8:9). If a person does not have the Spirit of God living on the inside, that person does not belong to God.

Jesus is responsible for giving the baptism of the Holy Spirit to those who will seek and receive Him. Jesus is also very excited to impart the gift of the baptism of the Holy Spirit because He understands that if a person does not partake of this glorious experience, that individual will not be able to enter into eternal life with Him. Jesus says in (Matthew 7:7-8) that to those who ask for what they desire, they will receive it; and to those who seek, they eventually will find what they are seeking for; and to those who knock, the door upon which they knock will be opened unto them.

The same good news holds true for those who desire to be filled with the Holy Spirit. If they ask, seek, and knock, they will not be disappointed in the process. It is important to understand that the baptism of the Holy Spirit is a gift that Jesus gives; therefore, this gift cannot be earned or labored for; it must simply be received through sincere faith and obedience.

When a person receives the Holy Spirit into their lives, they are literally given a brand-new heart! This new heart will be given to them because the old heart that they possess is diseased. In the Bible, the prophet Jeremiah summed up the old heart perfectly when he said that it was wicked and that no one could really know it (Jeremiah 17:9).

STEP 5

Speaking in Tongues

Thus far in our discussion, we have already underscored the importance of receiving the baptism of the Holy Spirit; however, another important matter must be addressed and that is: what evidence is there to prove that a man or woman has received the baptism of the Holy Spirit? We are constantly bombarded by people's religious opinions regarding the Holy Spirit and how He is to be received. However, if you are someone who loves and honors the teachings of the Bible which we have previously stated to be God's Word, you will not only look to man for understanding on this matter, but you will humbly turn your attention to the Bible and read it for yourself to see what it really teaches about receiving the Holy Spirit.

Again in (John 3:8) Jesus tells us about the baptism of the Holy Spirit and what will happen when this baptism occurs. Jesus compares the Holy Spirit to the wind. Like the wind, the Spirit is invisible; you cannot see it, neither can you tell where is comes from nor where it will go. But we are told that the evidence of the presence of the wind is its sound. So how will a person know for sure that he or she has received the baptism of the Spirit? They will hear a sound.

The very first time the baptism of the Holy Spirit was given; there were thousands of people who received it. However, as time went on, there were many thousands more who likewise received it. Of these many thousands, four of are given. For the sake of our discussion, we will consider two of them.

In (Acts 2:1-4), we are told that 120 people—both men and women—received this gift. This was the first time in the Bible the Holy Spirit was given to anyone. Luke, the writer of Acts, tells us that all the people who were present in the "upper room" were filled with the Holy Spirit, and subsequently all of them supernaturally began to speak in other tongues as God allowed them. This amazing experience is seen also in many other passages within this book, such as (Acts 10:44-46).

In the above passage, the Gentiles for the first time received the baptism of the Holy Spirit while they were listening to the Word of God preached to them by the Apostle Peter. Now the amazing thing to notice within this passage is that the people who came to listen as Peter preached were Jews. Yes, these people were the same individuals who had previously received the Holy Spirit back in chapter 2 of Acts.

These Jews were surprised that the gift which had been promised to them was also shared with non-Jewish individuals. How did they know that the Gentiles had also received the baptism of the Holy Spirit? What did they see? What did they hear? The scripture is clear: "for they heard them speak in tongues", and that was the exact experience that they had when they had received the baptism of the Holy Spirit (verse 46). It is no different today because God's plan for salvation has not changed.

THE JESUS NAME

Millions of people have been baptized all over the world in various ways. In (Matthew 28:19), Jesus told His disciples that they must go into the entire world and teach the Gospel to all people. He also told them that they should baptize all people in the name of the Father, and of the Son, and of the Holy Ghost? Why then is it that some churches teach that people who are water baptized must only be baptized in the name of Jesus?

The Plan for Salvation Questions

1. What is the meaning of the word conversion? (2 Corinthians 5:17)

2. Who is salvation for (Revelation 22:17)

3. Explain and discuss (2 Timothy 4:3-4)

4. Explain and discuss (Romans 3:3-4)

5. Explain and discuss (1 Peter 1:24-25)

6. Explain and discuss (Ephesians 4:5)

7. What is first needed from a person who intends of come to God? (Hebrews 11:6)

8. How does a person get faith? (Romans 10:17

9. Explain and discuss (James 2:14-17)

10. What two things did Jesus say should be preached in His name? (Luke 24:46-47)

11. Give the definition of repentance

12. Explain and discuss (2 Corinthians 7:10)

13. What did John request of those who came to be baptized of

him? (Luke 3:8)

14. What is promised to a person who is willing to ask God to forgive them of their sins? (1John 1:9)

15. Discuss (Romans 6:1)

16. Explain and discuss (1 Corinthians 6:9-10)

17. Explain and discuss (Romans 5:1)

18. What three experiences did Peter mention when he told the crowd what they needed to do in response to his message about Jesus? (Acts 2:38)

19. Explain and discuss (Romans 6:3-4)

20. What two things did Peter states about baptism? (1 Peter 3:21)

21. What was Paul told to have his sins washed away? (Acts 22:16)

22. How did Peter command those who had received the Holy Spirit to be baptized? (Acts 22:16)

23. Explain and discuss (Matthew 16:16)

24. When a person as but baptized in Jesus' name who do they put on? (Galatians 3:27)

25. Explain and discuss (Matthew 28:19)

26. Explain and discuss (Acts 4:10-12)

27. How did Jesus Christ receive His name? (Hebrews 1:4)

28. What does Isaiah tell us about Jesus? (Isaiah 9:6)

29. Who does Jesus say would send the Holy Spirit? (John 14:16)

30. Who does Jesus say would send the Holy Spirit? (John 15:26)

31. According to (John 14:18) who is the comforter?

32. Explain and discuss (Acts 19:1-5)

33. Explain and discuss (Acts 2:39)

34. Explain and discuss (Acts 2:1-4)

35. What special thing took place when these believers received the Holy Spirit?

36. Explain and discuss (John 3:1-8)

37. Discuss (Romans 8:9)

38. Discuss (Matthew 7:7-8)

39. Why it important that believers and given a new heart? (Jeremiah 17:9)

40. Explain and discuss (John 3:8)

41. What was the key sign that indicated that the gentiles had received the Holy Spirit? (Acts 10:44-46)

CHAPTER NINE
Benefits and Consequences

═══════════════════════════════════════

DISCUSSION 6

Now, in this our last discussion, we will look at the many wonderful benefits associated with accepting Jesus' offer of salvation. As well, we will examine the many negative consequences that those who choose to reject Jesus' offer of salvation will someday face. God has given to each human being the right to choose for themselves; this is otherwise known as *free will*. In the book of (Deuteronomy 30:19), God told the children of Israel that He was setting before them "life and death, blessing and cursing". God encouraged them to choose life, but He would not choose it for them.

God would simply stand at the door of their hearts and knock, patiently waiting, hoping that they would let Him in so that He could save them before their time ran out. This truth is seen today in (Revelation 3:20) where Jesus says, "Behold, I stand that the door and knock." Those who hear Him knocking, if they choose to, can open the door and let Jesus into their lives; Jesus will not open that door Himself because His is a perfect gentleman.

THE TRUTH ABOUT HEAVEN AND HELL

It is a known fact that people die every day. What happens to human beings when they die? Is life after death a real phenomenon? Are Heaven and Hell both real or are they myths?

Benefits and Consequences Questions

1. What two realities did God set before the children of Israel (Deuteronomy 30:19)

2. What was God's reason for giving this kind of free-will?

3. Discuss (Revelation 3:20)

4. What benefit will be given to the person who chooses to serve Jesus Christ? (John 3:16)

5. Discuss (John 14:1-3)

6. What privilege does John tell us what a believer is promised when he gives his life to Jesus? (John 1:12)

7. Explain and discuss (John 15:14)

8. What will be the end of those who did not hear or obey the plan for salvation? (1 Peter 4:17-18)

9. Explain and discuss (2 Thessalonians 1:8-9)

10. What is the appropriate time for a person's salvation? (2 Corinthians 6:2)

11. Explain and discuss (Hebrews 4:7)

12. Explain and discuss (Hebrews 9:27)

BENEFITS OF CHOOSING TO SERVE JESUS!

At this point, we will look specifically at some of the benefits that are associated with accepting Jesus Christ into one's life. First, when a person accepts Jesus, that person is given eternal life. The believer that faithfully lives for Him on Earth will live forever with Jesus in Heaven when He returns. Many passages in the Bible support this truth. In (John 3:16), Jesus told Nicodemus that anyone who believes in Him will "not perish" but will be given eternal life in the presence of Jesus Christ. (John 14:1-3) assures us of this.

A second benefit for the person who chooses to give their heart to Jesus is the privilege of becoming a son or a daughter of God. (John 1:12) explains that those who receive Jesus Christ's offering of salvation are given the right to become sons of God; wonderful news considering that they would have, before receiving Christ, been sons and daughters of the Devil. To be considered as one of God's sons or daughters is a high privilege. It means that you are not a stranger anymore (Ephesians 2:19) and that you have access to all that your Heavenly Father has to offer. Not only will you have access to what He offers in Heaven but you will have access to what He offers right here on earth. And mostly importantly, He now considers you a friend as John tells us in (John 15:14).

NEGATIVE CONSEQUENCES

On the other hand, those who choose to reject Jesus' offer of salvation will not share in the benefits of those that have. One day, the apostle Peter asked an important question! He asked what would happen to those people who did not hear or obey the message of the Gospel (1 Peter 4:17-18). Paul gave a shocking response to Peter's question in (2 Thessalonians 1:8-9) where he stated that those who do not know God or obey God's Gospel would be afflicted by fire. By

Peter's question and Paul's response, we can clearly see how important it is for people to seek to know Jesus and to accept Him as their Lord and Savior. Those who do not do so will not only live unfulfilled lives while here on earth, but in their life after death they will live forever in the lake of fire.

There are many reasons why individuals may decide that they are not ready to give their lives over to God. Perhaps they have heard the gospel but due to the fact that they are in a relationship with someone who there are not married to or are perhaps practicing some other type of sin, they figure that they will wait until they have given up that sin before they serve Jesus Christ. However, if the truth be told, procrastination is a great deceiver because no one knows the day or the hour that their number will be called for them to leave this earth. Some people are blessed with a long life span while others get only a few short years, months or even days, of life on earth.

It is not a wise thing to put off serving Jesus Christ because tomorrow is never promised to any one no matter how young or how healthy. The Bible tells us clearly that today is the day of salvation (2 Corinthians 6:2); now is the appropriate time to serve God. In another passage, we are told that a person must choose not to harden their hearts (Hebrews 4:7).

As was previously stated, all human beings have an appointment with death. In (Hebrews 9:27), Paul tells us that it is appointed unto men to at least die once, but after his death Paul says that there will come a judgment which John tells us of in (Revelation 20:11-15). Here in Revelation, we are told of what will ultimately happen at the end. We are assured by the Word of God that no man or woman will be able to boycott this day. All must stand and give an account for how they chose to live the life that God gave them to live. While

Jesus Christ was here on earth, He asked His disciples a question that I believe is needful for us to ask as well (Matthew 16:26).

If I were to paraphrase what Jesus asked, I would say it like this: what would have been the purpose of our lives here on earth if we had managed to gain the entire world, but in the process, had lost our souls? What of earths many offers are so attractive or even enjoyable that they would cause a person to forfeit coming to Jesus Christ for salvation? In (1 John 2:15-17), John tells us all that is present in the world to hinder us.

Again if I were to paraphrase what he said, I would say: do not give your love, time, youth, or devotion to the world because all you will find in the world is the lust of the flesh, then the lust of the eyes, and finally the pride of life. Therefore, it is not worth trading Jesus for the world because one day the world will be no more and none of the many things that you see in the world now will last; they will one day come to lose their value and attraction.

No excuse will be sufficient on the Day of Judgment because God has given all of us a fair chance to both hear and respond of the Gospel. It is the love of God that moves Him to allow us to hear the Gospel. It is sad to note that some people only hear about God's love once before they die, while others hear about Jesus Christ and His love for them on a daily basis.

What will your response be after you hear of all that God has done for you? Will you be a wise person and humbly receive Jesus Christ into your life and be saved, or will you be foolish and reject Him and make your eternal home in the lake of fire. Jesus tells of the story in (Matthew 7:24-27) of two builders, one who was foolish and the other wise. The wise builder built his house upon a rock and when the winds blew on his house and rain descended upon it, that house was able to withstand it all.

However, the foolish builder built his house upon the sand, and when the winds blew and the rain descended upon his house, it experienced a great fall. Those who receive Jesus will be secure in all their troubles, while those who do not will have their life end in doom. In (2 Peter 3:9), Peter tells us about God's desire for the salvation of human beings. He says that it is not God's will that any person perish, but rather God desires to see all people come to repentance.

Finally, I will conclude this discussion by saying that rejecting Jesus Christ does not have to be done verbally, because to reject Jesus is as simple as hearing about His love and His offer of salvation and simply fail to act on the goodness He offers. How does a person get their name into the book of life? The answer to this question is simple! One *must* obey the plan of salvation.

13. Explain and discuss (Revelation 20:11-15)

14. Explain and discuss (Matthew 16:26)

15. What are the three things that are in the world? (1 John 2:15-17)

16. Explain and discuss (Matthew 7:24-27)

17. Explain and discuss (2 Peter 3:9)

CONCLUSION

The conclusion of this discussion is designed for those who will be teaching this study. I would like to challenge each and every one of you to aim at conducting this discussion with at least one person each month. The primary goal of this discussion is to help God's people to fulfill the "Great Commission" which Jesus has left for us to do here on earth while we still have the strength to serve Him. Many people say that they are not very comfortable with sharing their faith. They state that, very often, when they are engaged in conversations at work, school, on the street or elsewhere, they simply do not always know what to say or how to correctly answer questions.

In (2 Peter 3:15), Peter tells us that we should "always be ready to give an answer when someone asks" us what we believe. Therefore, because of this, it is vitally important that we are all aware of the Word of God even if what we know is as simple as what is presented in this book. It is also important that we are able to share the Word of God in a manner that those whom we share it with will be able to understand it and eventually make the all-important decision of serving Jesus Christ. My brothers and sisters, we are told by Jesus in (Matthew 5:13) that we are to be like "the salt of the earth" to the world and in the following verse; Jesus also tells us that we are to be a "light" to the world.

These are two very important responsibilities for all of us to participate in—being salt and light. Notwithstanding, a greater percentage of us are not acting like "light" or like "salt" in the world. For many years now, it appears that many of us have become stuck in the salt shaker, so to speak, and have not fully allowed ourselves to be used by God to positively impact the lives of people whom we deal with on a daily basis. Many of the people that we interact with, unfortunately, do not know that we are followers of Christ.

They do not know that within us lie the answers to many of their questions. They do not know that within us, by virtue of being children of God, the Word of God rests in our hearts and that very Word which we are empowered to speak about, has the power to save them and give their lives greater meaning and purpose. They do not know these things because our mouths are sealed and we are afraid that perhaps if we open our mouths, we might not know what to say.

That is not what Jesus expects from us. His Word says that when He gave us the gift of the Holy Spirit, He also gave us power! He gave us power for one primary reason, and that reason is to be witnesses on His behalf; to tell people all over the world about His love, His grace, and His message of salvation. One question that so many of us must answer is whether or not we are using that power we have been given for its intended purpose. Are we reaching out to people who are not saved with the message of hope? Are we fulfilling the Great Commission?

The truth is brothers and sisters; we have so little time left before the Lord Jesus Christ is set to return, not to mention the short time left of our own existence on Earth. When we face the Lord during our judgment, He will ask us what we did with our time as far as evangelism and soul-winning are concerned. What will we tell Him? Will we tell Him what we tell our pastors and church leaders; that we were busy, or that we had to work or attend class or some other social event? He would not accept such excuses because He knows the truth.

According to one reputable source, it is estimated that there are 6,446,131,400 people on the planet. However, out of this large populace, roughly 1.8 people die per second, 108 people die per minute, 6,480 people die per hour; which would result in 155, 520 people dying each day. If we would continue to observe these figures, one can conclude, that 1,088,640 people die each week. What is most shocking and even heart-breaking about this is that the greater percentage of these people who have died are going to Hell because they did not obey the Gospel or perhaps did not hear it at all. Would it not be terrible if any of these people who died and did not hear the Gospel message of hope were those who lived in our communities or even on our streets?

I say all of this to say that we all have a great assignment to accomplish together, and a short time to do it. So, as I encourage you I also encourage myself. Let us run, from this day forward, understanding that we are Christ's hands, mouth, and feet. We have a mission to fulfill, and we are not doing this on our own; Christ will help us. Starting today, let us determine to "Teach for Souls".

ABOUT THE AUTHOR

Clinton Taylor has been a teacher of the Bible for more than a decade, both in Canada and in other parts of the world. He is currently studying history at a local university in Ontario and he is committed to carrying out Christ's mission by focusing on the areas of soul winning by assisting congregations in implementing strategies for numeric and spiritual growth.

LaVergne, TN USA
22 September 2009
158579LV00001B/23/P